TIMELESS TALES

Tall Tales

Retold by TANA REIFF

Illustrated by BILL BAYLIS

NEW READERS PRESS

Library of Congress Cataloging-in-Publication Data

Reiff, Tana.
Tall tales / retold by Tana Reiff;
illustrated by Bill Baylis. p. cm. — (Timeless tales)
ISBN 0-88336-463-8
1. Readers for new literates. 2. Tall tales.
I. Baylis, Bill. II. Title.
III. Series: Reiff, Tana. Timeless tales.
PE1126.A4R447   1993
428.6'2—dc20   93-16084
                                     CIP
                                     AC

Contents

Introduction

Have you ever told a story that went past the truth? You weren't really telling a lie; you were telling a tall tale.

People all over the world have told tall tales for years. Such stories make people laugh. The tales grow taller, and farther from the truth, each time they are told.

Many folks think of tall tales as American. After all, a big, new country has a lot of room for big stories. But America isn't the only place where tall tales are told. In this book you'll read four tall tales from the United States and one Native American tall tale. You'll read some tall tales from other countries too.

Many tall tales are about giants. Some of the most famous are Paul Bunyan, Stormalong, John Henry, and the silly Irish giants you'll read about here. They can do things that other people can't, because they are so large.

Giants aren't the only ones who do amazing things. The cowboy Pecos Bill is no giant, but he has special powers.

The story tellers from Burma and Syria are not giants or people with special powers. They just enjoy telling wild stories. Others enjoyed hearing them, and now you can enjoy them, too.

Paul Bunyan, the Lumberjack

United States and Canada

 Paul Bunyan was the most famous
lumberjack ever. He was born big.
As he grew bigger and bigger,
he needed Something Big to do
in a Big Way.

Paul tried hunting. He was *too* big for that line of work. He found that out the time he shot a bear. Paul went to see where the bear fell. With his long legs he got to the bear before the bullet did. You know what happened? Paul got that bullet in his own rear end!

Paul found his best friend, Babe the Blue Ox, during the Winter of the Blue Snow. Babe stood up and started kicking over trees as if they were toothpicks. That's when Paul knew what kind of work he should do. He decided to clear trees to build the new land of America. This would become his life's work.

He and Babe became a team. Paul would swing his axe. The tree would fall. Then Babe would pull out the stump.

Paul began to set up lumber camps all across the country. He put a lot of people to work cutting down trees. Of course, no one was faster or stronger than Paul Bunyan himself.

Feeding all those hungry lumberjacks was a problem. They could eat hundreds and hundreds of pancakes. The cook, Hot Biscuit Slim, couldn't make enough pancakes in his little pans.

"I have an idea!" Paul called to the cook. Paul's voice was very loud. Three men were knocked over by the sound.

Paul got a blacksmith to make a big, round pancake griddle. It was a mile wide. The question was how to get that griddle over to the lumber camp.

"No problem!" said Paul in his big voice. He turned the heavy iron griddle on its edge. Then he rolled it along like a giant silver dollar. He rolled it the whole way to the lumber camp.

Next, Paul tied slabs of bacon to the feet of the cookhouse boys. Those boys skated across the griddle. In no time at all, it was greased up and ready.

Hot Biscuit Slim got to work. He made pancakes so big it took five men to eat one. Paul could eat one big pancake all by himself. The pancake problem was fixed.

The next problem came up at a camp in Michigan. There wasn't enough room to store drinking water for all the lumberjacks. So Paul dug out a hole to store rain water. It wasn't big enough. He dug another hole. Still not enough. In the end, Paul dug out five great big holes. Today, they are called the Great Lakes. That's one way Paul Bunyan changed the map.

Another map change happened the time Babe got sick. Paul heard about springs of water in Wyoming. Drinking this water was supposed to make sick people well. So Paul took Babe to Wyoming.

Paul began to dig for a spring. He dug so deep, he dropped his shovel. It fell for an hour before he heard it hit. Then, all of a sudden the shovel came flying out of the ground. It flew up on a pole of steam. That iron shovel got so hot, it melted.

An hour later, steam came shooting from the ground again. The next hour it happened again. As a matter of fact, Paul had found what everyone now calls Old Faithful. Ever since, it shoots up hot steam every hour. People from far and wide go to Wyoming to get a look.

And what about Babe? Well, he just got sicker. Paul decided to take him to California. Maybe some good weather would make the ox well again.

By the time they got to Utah, Paul thought Babe was almost dead. He started digging a grave. He cried as he dug, thinking about life without his best friend. He cried so many big, salty tears into that hole that it became the Great Salt Lake.

After that, Paul and Babe headed across Arizona. Paul carried Babe on his shoulders and dragged his axe behind him. The axe was so big, it left a deep mark. It was a ditch, really. Pretty soon people started calling that ditch the Grand Canyon.

The story of Paul Bunyan is a story without an end. Years later, Babe did die. That's when Paul decided his lumberjack days were over. Times had changed. Paul didn't feel needed anymore. So one night Paul just walked out of camp. No one saw him go. He never came back.

Paul Bunyan still lives somewhere out in the woods. He won't die till the last tree is cut down. And a good many people hope that will never happen.

Pecos Bill, the Cowboy

United States

Nobody saw baby Bill fall out of the covered wagon. It happened in Texas, near the Pecos River. His family was heading west. They had so many children that they didn't know the baby was gone till two days later.

A family of coyotes found baby Bill and raised him like one of their own. Bill didn't even know he was a person till Cowboy Chuck came along. It turned out Bill and Chuck were brothers. Chuck knew this when he spotted the blue star on Bill's arm. Everyone in the family had a blue star, like their pa.

Well, Chuck took Bill back to the ranch he had set up in Texas. Everyone started calling him Pecos Bill because of where he had been lost. Pretty soon, Bill became a cowboy.

Living with the coyotes had made Bill pretty quick, and tough too. So it wasn't long before Bill became the best cowpoke on the ranch. The other cowboys had some pretty poor ways of doing things. Take the way they roped a <u>steer.</u> They would lay out a rope in a circle on the ground. Then they would hide behind

a tree and wait for a steer to come along. When the steer walked into the circle they would pull on the rope to tie him in.

Bill had a better way. He called it a lasso. He would loop the rope and swing it around in the air. He would ride right up to a steer and toss that rope around its neck.

So Bill invented the lasso. He also invented branding, six-shooters, spurs, round-ups, and the rodeo. As a matter of fact, Pecos Bill taught cowboys just about everything cowboys do. Even how to <u>yodel</u>, which he learned from the coyotes.

14

There's a good story about how Bill got his famous horse. It was a mustang, gold in color and wild as they come. Bill made a great big slingshot. He got the cowboys to shoot him into the air. When he came down, he landed right in front of the mustang. The horse stopped short and got his front feet stuck in the ground. Bill jumped on the mustang's back and pulled him out. The horse was so happy to be free that he turned around and gave Bill a big kiss.

Bill never broke that wild horse, really. See, only Bill could ride him. The horse would throw anyone else. They would fall to the ground and break their necks. That's why folks started calling Bill's horse Widow-Maker.

Out west you see a lot of canyons. A canyon is a deep valley with steep sides. Bill and Widow-Maker enjoyed jumping across the canyons. Together, they could almost fly.

Soon, jumping the little canyons got too easy. Bill decided to try jumping the Grand Canyon, the biggest one of all. He and Widow-Maker took off into the air. Bill waited for the sound of Widow-Maker's feet hitting the other side. He waited and waited. "I guess it takes longer to jump the Grand Canyon," Bill said to himself. But he kept on waiting and still didn't hear Widow-Maker landing.

Then Bill looked down. He saw the ground below getting bigger. He knew that meant it was getting closer. And if the ground was getting closer, then that meant he and Widow-Maker were falling!

"WHOA!" Bill shouted to Widow-Maker. You must know that Widow-Maker *always* listened to Bill. So when Bill said "WHOA!" Widow-Maker stopped, even when he was in mid-air.

"That was a close call!" laughed Bill. "Now we gotta finish the job we started." Widow-Maker made another jump. It was just long enough to land on the other side. "We did it, buddy!" said Bill. "We had to do it in two parts, but we jumped the Grand Canyon!"

Bill never forgot the first time he saw his true love, Slue-foot Sue. She was riding a catfish in the river. "There's the gal I want to marry!" Bill said.

Slue-foot Sue looked over at Bill. "You're the best cowboy I ever did see!" she said. "You're the fellow I want to marry!"

"It's a deal!" said Bill.

They planned a big wedding, fancy white dress and all. When Sue showed up in that dress, everyone just stopped in their tracks. It was the most beautiful dress in the world. It had a big bustle—that's a thing that makes the back of a skirt stick up. This bustle was held together with a spring.

"Now y'all saw me as a beautiful bride," said Sue. "I'll take my leave from y'all and I'll be right back."

She ran off. In a few minutes she came back in cowgirl clothes. She must have had those clothes on under the wedding dress. She forgot one thing, however. She had left on the bustle.

Wanting to make a big show, she hopped onto Widow-Maker. But—and Sue should have known this would happen—the horse bucked her into the air. All the cowboys took off their hats to watch Sue bounce up into the sky.

They kept on watching. It wasn't till an hour and a half later that she came back down. But as soon as that steel-spring bustle hit the ground, Sue bounced right back up. This went on all day. Up and down, up and down, with an hour and a half in between.

The next day, Sue was *still* bouncing, but not as high. Now it took only an hour to come back down.

By the third day, Sue was *still* bouncing. "Why don't you do something about this?" everyone asked Pecos Bill.

Bill did want to marry
Sue. And he was tired
of waiting for his
bouncing bride to stay
on the ground. So he
did what any good
cowboy would do.
The next time Sue came
down, Bill lassoed her.
As soon as she got on
her feet, he pulled off that stupid bustle and
married her on the spot.

Pecos Bill and Slue-foot Sue were a happy
pair. They raised a bunch of kids, and a
bunch of coyotes, too.

John Henry, the Natural Man

United States

 He was born a slave, John Henry was. And folks down South say he was born with a hammer in his hand. "He's going to be a natural man," his daddy said.

As a small child, John Henry picked cotton like the other slaves. But he could pick more than the grown folks. No one had ever picked more than one bale in a day. John Henry picked at least three bales each and every day! "I'm just a natural man," he would say.

After the slaves became free, John Henry headed west. He wanted to find his true calling. He didn't know where he would stop.

One day he heard a ringing far away. The more he walked, the closer he got to the sound. Then he saw what it was. A gang of men was building a railroad. Their hammers rang like bells as they pounded spikes into the track.

"I've found my calling," John Henry said at once. "I want to be a steel-driving man!"

John Henry was about 10 times bigger than any other man. But he went to work right along with the little guys. Only three strikes of the hammer was all it took for him to drive a spike. Soon, he started using two hammers at once, one in each hand. He got more done than six other men working real fast. On top of that, he sang while he worked.

One time, the gang was laying track when some news came. The 5:15 train would be coming right on time. They would have to hurry to finish the track before the train got there.

"Everyone out of the way!" John Henry called out. He grabbed 100 feet of track and rolled it up. He swung that roll of track around over his head and let it go. It landed in a beautiful straight line.

Next, he stuffed about three dozen spikes into his mouth. He spit them out, two at a time. With a hammer in each hand, he hammered in both spikes at once. He heard the whistle of the 5:15 train getting close. There was no time to waste.

In a flash, he hammered in the last two spikes. Then he jumped back off the track. The 5:15 tore past. John Henry had finished that track just in time!

Everyone clapped and patted John Henry on the back. (Really, they could only reach his knees.) "I'm just a natural man," he said.

John Henry is best remembered for his race against the steam drill. The steam drill was a new machine. It was supposed to take the place of people.

"Who's faster—man or machine?" John Henry's boss wanted to know. "I want you to race that steam drill," he told John Henry.

So John Henry set himself up on the right side of the track. The steam drill was set up on the left side of the track. The starting gun went off. "Begin!" shouted the boss.

John Henry worked like crazy. The steam drill plugged along at high speed. After the first hour, the steam drill was ahead. John Henry's hammers were getting hot from moving so fast. The men threw water on them to cool them down.

After the second hour, the steam drill was still ahead, but not by much. John Henry's hammers were red hot now. The men threw more water on them so they wouldn't catch on fire.

After the third hour, man and machine were both getting tired. The steam drill broke down and had to be fixed. That gave John Henry a chance to catch up.

With ten minutes to go, the race was close. Strong as he was, John Henry was slowing down. He felt himself falling behind. He put his mind on his wife Polly and his fine children. He started to sing. He worked harder than he ever had before.

The race ended with the ring of a bell. John Henry looked up. He had beaten the steam drill by four feet! Then a terrible thing happened. John Henry dropped his hammer. He fell to the ground. The natural man was dead.

There's a song about John Henry. It ends like this:

> He drove so hard that he broke his poor heart,
>
> And laid down his hammer and he died, Oh, Lord!
>
> And laid down his hammer and he died.

Stormalong, the Sailor

United States

A. B. Stormalong was a great man of the sea. In fact, he was probably the greatest sailor of all time. When he was born, the A. B. stood for Alfred Bulltop. That changed when he first signed on to work on a sailing ship. He was so large, the captain looked at him and said, "Now there's an Able-Bodied seaman if I ever did see one!"

A. B. Stormalong was born during the biggest hurricane Cape Cod had ever seen.

That hurricane was just a taste of the life ahead for Stormalong.

He was born with blue and green eyes, just like the sea, and they stayed that way. The baby was so big, he played with the sharks in the ocean as if they were other kids.

By the age of 12, he had to leave school because he was too big to fit into the school house. It was time for Stormalong to do what he always wanted—go to sea. He went down to the dock. There, the captain of the *Lady of the Sea* asked him a few questions.

"Suppose a big storm kicked up on the ship's starboard side," the captain asked. "What would you do?"

"I'd drop the anchor," Stormalong answered.

"Suppose another big storm kicked up at the ship's stern," the captain went on. "What would you do?"

26

"I'd drop the anchor," Stormalong answered again.

"Suppose another big storm kicked up on the port side," the captain said. "What would you do?"

"I'd drop the anchor," Stormalong answered again.

"Suppose another big storm kicked up off the prow," the captain said. "What would you do?"

"I'd drop the anchor," Stormalong answered yet again.

"Now, let me ask you this," said the captain. "Where did you get all those anchors you would drop?"

"Same place you got all those storms," said Stormalong.

"Hey, you're pretty sharp!" said the captain. "I'll take you on."

Stormalong set sail on the *Lady of the Sea,* which carried cargo back and forth across the Atlantic Ocean. The young man did a fine job, and he kept at it for the next few years. But he didn't feel right for one minute, going or coming. That's because the ship was just too small for the big guy.

So the next time the *Lady of the Sea* came to Cape Cod, Stormalong did what he felt was the right thing to do. He took up the anchor and swallowed it whole. To swallow the anchor showed that he was finished at sea.

Grabbing one oar from the ship, Stormalong headed west on foot. He carried the oar over his back. He made up his mind not to stop walking till someone asked him what it was. That way, he would know he was far from the sea. Somewhere in Iowa, an old man along the road finally said, "What is that thing?" That's the spot where Stormalong started his farm.

He didn't last long as a farmer. All he could think about was the sea. So he headed back east, back to the port. He couldn't believe his eyes when he saw what was there. It was the biggest ship in the world! "Stormalong!" shouted one of the men on deck. "We built this ship so you could sail along!"

Some room to move around was all Stormalong needed. So off he went on this big new ship. It was called the *Courser.* The men made Stormalong the captain.

The *Courser* sailed across the ocean. But between France and England a big problem came up. The English Channel, between the two countries, is 21 miles wide. That's only two inches wider than the *Courser*. On one side were the Dark Cliffs of Dover. It would be a mighty tight fit past those cliffs.

It so happened that the *Courser*'s cargo was soap. Tons of it. "Only one thing to do!" Stormalong told his sailors. He sent half the crew out in lifeboats. The other half swung from ropes down the sides of the ship. Everyone rubbed soap all over the ship. "Lay it on thick!" Stormalong called to the men.

Getting past those cliffs was no problem at all. With all that soap on it, the ship slid through like a fish. Not only that, the soap rubbed off on the cliffs. That's why today they are called the White Cliffs of Dover.

As the *Courser* got back close to home, a big storm kicked up. There was so much rain and wind, it made Stormalong think of the night he was born. You couldn't see two feet. "Where are we?" the sailors asked.

One of the sailors dropped a line into the water. When he pulled it up, the lead weight on the end had some cabbage stuck on it. Stormalong knew right where the ship was. "Why, I smell Mrs. Jones's cabbage patch!" he said. "We're right over my home town on Cape Cod!"

The next morning, back on land,
Stormalong ran into Mrs. Jones herself.
"I had a strange dream last night," she said.
"There was a big storm. There was so much
rain that Cape Cod was under water. I
dreamed that your ship sailed right over
my cabbage patch!"

"Well, you were right," said Stormalong.
He was not one bit surprised.

The Tall-Tale Tellers

Burma

 There once were three brothers who loved to tell tall tales. "We don't believe a word you say!" the people of their village would shout. Then someone would beg to hear another story.

One day the three brothers went out on the road. They stood ready to tell a story to anyone who passed by. Along came a prince. He was dressed in fine clothes and bright jewels. The brothers whispered among themselves, "Wouldn't it be nice to have these rich things for ourselves?" They made a plan.

As the prince came near, the first brother spoke to him. "Sit down with us and rest," he said. "Let us each tell a story about something we did in the past. Anyone who does not believe another's story must become his slave."

The brothers did not want to make the prince their slave. However, a slave must turn over everything he owns. If the prince became a slave, the brothers would get his clothes and jewels.

"Very well," said the prince. "You go first."

The first brother began his tale. "Before I was born, I was taking a walk in the woods. I spotted a fruit tree. The fruit looked so good that I just had to have some. So I climbed the tree. I ate so much fruit that I felt too heavy to climb back down. I had to go back to town and get a rope. Then I climbed down the rope and went home."

Of course, this story never could have happened. But did anyone say they didn't believe the first brother? No. No one wanted to become a slave.

The second brother spoke next. "When I was a week old, I too took a walk in the woods. I was minding my own business. Then I spotted a tiger. I knew he would spring at me and kill me. So as the tiger opened his mouth, I jumped in. Inside the tiger I jumped up and down. I made loud noises. I really scared him. Then I jumped back out and broke the tiger in half."

The prince and the other two brothers knew this story could not be true. Yet, no one said so.

The third brother went next. "When I was one year old, I was taking a walk along the river. I saw people trying to catch fish. No one was catching a thing. Not even a bite. They all looked very sad. So I went into the water to find out why no one was catching fish. I turned into a fish and swam around for three days.

"At last I spotted the problem. A huge fish down there was eating every little fish that passed his way. Just as the fish tried to eat me too, I turned back into a person. I cut open the big fish. Out came hundreds of little fish. As I came out of the water, the people by the river were catching millions of fish. It was all because of me."

No one said a word.

It was the prince's turn to tell a story. "I am a very rich prince. I am out today looking for three slaves who ran away from me. I am so happy that I found you three brothers, for now I have found my slaves!"

The brothers knew they were in trouble. Anyone who said they did not believe the prince's story would become a slave. If they did not speak up, they would have to go with the prince and become slaves anyway. None of the brothers spoke.

"You are now my slaves!" laughed the prince. "Give me your clothes and I will set you free!"

The three tall-tale tellers had no choice. They took off their clothes, gave them to the prince, and walked back to town as bare as babies.

That was the last time the three brothers ever told tall tales. From that day on, everything they said was the simple truth.

Oona
and the
Giants

Ireland

A long time ago, in Ireland, there lived more than a few giants. Every one of them was strong. But not every giant was brave.

One of those not-very-brave ones was named Fingal. He was most afraid of another giant, named Cucullin. For years, Cucullin wanted to fight Fingal. Cucullin looked all over the land for Fingal. All those years, Fingal kept out of Cucullin's way.

All of Cucullin's strength was in the middle finger of his right hand. Everyone in Ireland knew about that middle finger, even Fingal.

Fingal had a rather magic finger himself. When he sucked his thumb, he could "see" what would happen before it happened. People would laugh to see a huge man like Fingal sucking his thumb. That is why he did it only when he was at home with his very smart wife, Oona.

One day, Fingal was sucking his thumb. All of a sudden he yelled, "Oh, no! Oona, my thumb tells me that Cucullin has found me! He is on his way to get me! What am I going to do?"

"Don't worry," said Oona. "I'll take care of him."

First, Oona went around to all the neighbors. She borrowed all the flat iron pans she could find. She brought them all home.

Oona made three huge pancakes with pans cooked inside them. After that, she made three more plain pancakes, with no pans inside them.

"How is all this cooking going to save me from Cucullin?" Fingal wanted to know.

"You will see," Oona told him.

"My thumb tells me that Cucullin is getting very close," said Fingal. "He is coming up the hill to our house right now!"

"Very well," said Oona. "See that baby cradle over there? The one you made for the baby we will have someday?"

Fingal looked over at the cradle. "Yes," he said. "I see it."

Oona handed Fingal some baby clothes. "Put these on and get yourself into that cradle," she said.

Fingal climbed into the cradle. It was a tight fit. Then Oona tied a baby cap onto Fingal's very large head. "You look sweet!" she told him.

Oona and Fingal heard Cucullin's big steps coming close to the door. The ground shook. Cucullin knocked three times. Oona answered the door as if nothing were wrong. Fingal watched from the cradle, sucking his thumb.

"Where's Fingal?" Cucullin asked.

"He went out after some little giant named Cucullin," said Oona. "I hope that poor man is ready for the likes of my husband. I don't even want to tell you what he will do to him! It won't be pretty."

"I am Cucullin," said Cucullin.

"Well, if I were you, I would keep away from my husband," said Oona. "He would be the end of you!"

Just then, a strong wind blew in the front door.

"That's a cold wind," said Oona. "Fingal would go out and turn the house around, away from the wind. Say, you look pretty strong. Would you mind turning the house around, since Fingal isn't home?"

Cucullin went outside. He picked up the house and turned it around, away from the wind.

"Can't thank you enough," said Oona. "Say, we need some water. Fingal gets water from a spring under that large rock out there. Since he isn't home, would you mind lifting up the rock?"

Cucullin went out and pulled on his middle finger. He lifted the huge rock and brought Oona some water.

"Thank you," said Oona. "Would you care for some nice, fresh cakes? I just made them."

"I am sort of hungry," said Cucullin. But when he bit into the first cake, he hit the iron pan in the middle. He spit out the cake and two teeth along with it. "Does Fingal eat these cakes?" he asked.

"He can't get enough of them!" said Oona.

"CAKE! CAKE!" called Fingal from the cradle.

"My, that's a big baby," said Cucullin.

"Takes after his father," said Oona. She gave Fingal one of the plain cakes. He ate it with no problem at all. Then he cried for more.

"I can't believe the baby can eat that cake," said Cucullin. "What kind of teeth does he have?"

"See for yourself," said Oona.

Cucullin put the middle finger of his right hand into the baby's mouth. He felt way back in. Before Cucullin knew what was happening, Fingal bit that special finger right off.

Cucullin screamed in pain. He ran out of the house without saying goodbye. He headed down the windy hill, and was never seen again.

Not long after, Oona and Fingal had a real baby. He was big, all right, as he rocked in that cradle. And when he sucked his thumb, he looked just like his father.

Nothing but Lies

Syria

 The world's greatest storyteller lived many years ago. His name was Abu Nuwas. He could tell long stories, one after another, and never tell the same story twice.

Word of Abu reached the ruler of the land. He ordered Abu to his palace. "I hear of your story telling," said the ruler. "You tell true stories, do you?"

"Mostly true," said Abu. "Sometimes I add a little something to make a story interesting."

"I dare you to tell me a story that holds not one word of truth," said the ruler.

"That will not be easy," said Abu. "But for you, I will do anything. To begin my story, I must say I am my father's brother."

"So far, so good," the ruler said with a smile.

"When I was young, I took care of my father," Abu went on. "One day I took him to the bazaar.* There, we bought one egg. As we carried it home, a chick popped out of the egg. While we walked on, the chick grew and grew. It grew so large that my father and I climbed onto the chicken's back and rode it home."

Bazaar is the Arabic word for street market.

The ruler laughed to think of a chicken big enough to ride on.

"We kept the chicken as a pet," said Abu. "But she ate us out of house and home. We decided to find work for the chicken to pay for her own food. So she began carrying wood for people. This made her back very sore. To help the chicken feel better, we rubbed her back with nut oil. This made

the chicken's back well again. However, the next day a nut tree grew out of the chicken's back."

The ruler laughed to think of a chicken with a tree growing out of her back.

Abu went on with his tall tale. "In a week, a crop of nuts had grown on the tree. It took us a whole week to pick all those nuts. When we were finished we found the chicken had gone to sleep in the tree. So we threw mud at her to wake her up. That mud began to spread! You never saw such a sight! The mud spread out and made a whole new farm. All of a sudden we had 40 acres of new ground."

"Go on," said the ruler. "This is getting good."

"Well, we put our cows on our new farm," said Abu. "Then my father and I planted sesame seeds up there. But nothing grew. My grandfather told us to plant something else instead. So my father and I picked up all the sesame seeds we could find. There was one seed we could not find. Then we spotted an ant dragging that one sesame seed toward his hill. We got into a tug-of-war with the ant. And do you know what happened?"

"I couldn't guess!" laughed the ruler.

"The sesame seed broke in half," said Abu. "So much oil flowed out of that little seed that it made a new river. To get away from the oil, we jumped into my grandfather's hollow tooth. We stayed there for 40 days. We lived off the sheep my father had brought along into the tooth."

"Then what happened?" the ruler asked.

"Lucky for us, my father had also brought along a rope," said Abu. "We climbed down the rope and landed safe and sound on the ground. And that is the end of my story."

"Is your story true or false?" asked the ruler.

"Why, it was true, of course," said Abu.

"But I wanted a story that held not one word of truth," said the ruler.

"I'm getting good at lying," said Abu. "I only said it was true to keep up my big lie!"

The ruler was very pleased. He gave Abu 40 pieces of gold, one for each acre of false ground and each day spent in the hollow tooth.